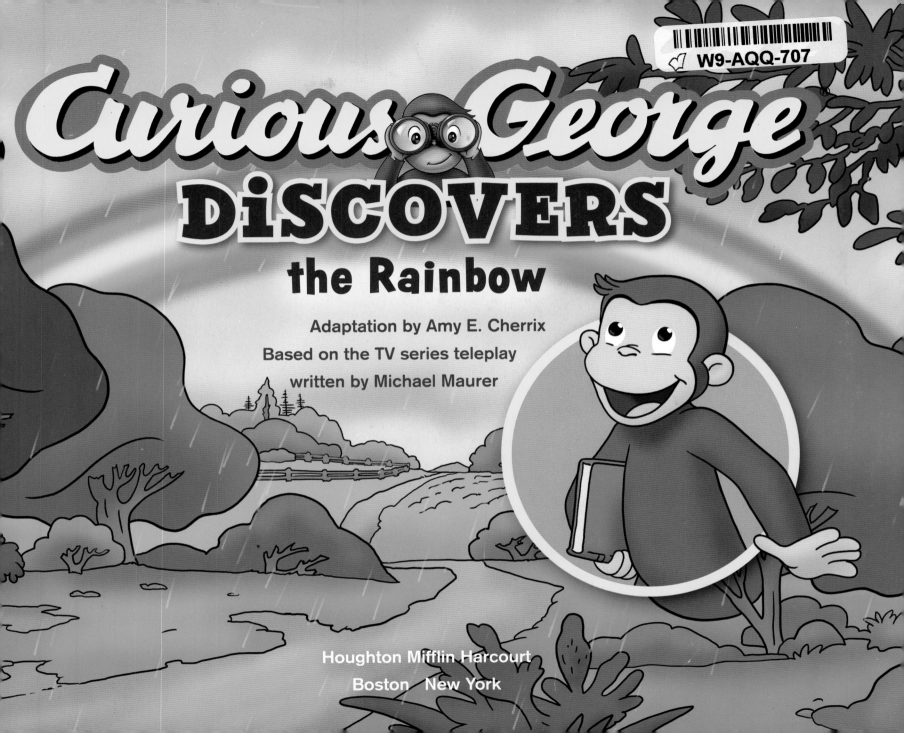

Curious George DiSCOVERS the Rainbow

Adaptation by Amy E. Cherrix

Based on the TV series teleplay
written by Michael Maurer

Houghton Mifflin Harcourt

Boston   New York

Photographs on cover (bottom) and 15, 22, 24, 32 courtesy of HMH/Carrie Garcia

Photograph on p. 3 courtesy of HMH/Mark Picard

Photograph on p. 7 courtesy of HMH/Guy Jarvis

Top photograph on p. 8 ©Sonny Senser/Houghton Mifflin Harcourt

Middle photograph on p. 8 ©Sam Dudgeon/Houghton Mifflin Harcourt

Photograph on p.9 ©George Winkler/Houghton Mifflin Harcourt

All other images ©Houghton Mifflin Harcourt

ISBN: 978-0-544-45425-5 paper over board
ISBN: 978-0-544-43068-6 paperback

Design by Susanna Vagt
www.hmhco.com
Printed in China
SCP 10 9 8 7 6 5 4 3 2 1
4500515588

George was a good little monkey and always very curious. Sometimes curiosity gets a good little monkey lost in the woods—especially when he's chasing leprechauns. Would you believe that that's how George discovered the rainbow? And it all started on a bright sunny day.

It was a beautiful day in the country. Steve and Betsy were visiting from the city for the first time. George couldn't wait for their outdoor adventure to begin. But first they had to unpack. When Betsy dropped her books, George rushed to help her pick them up. That's when he saw something he had never seen before . . . something amazing.

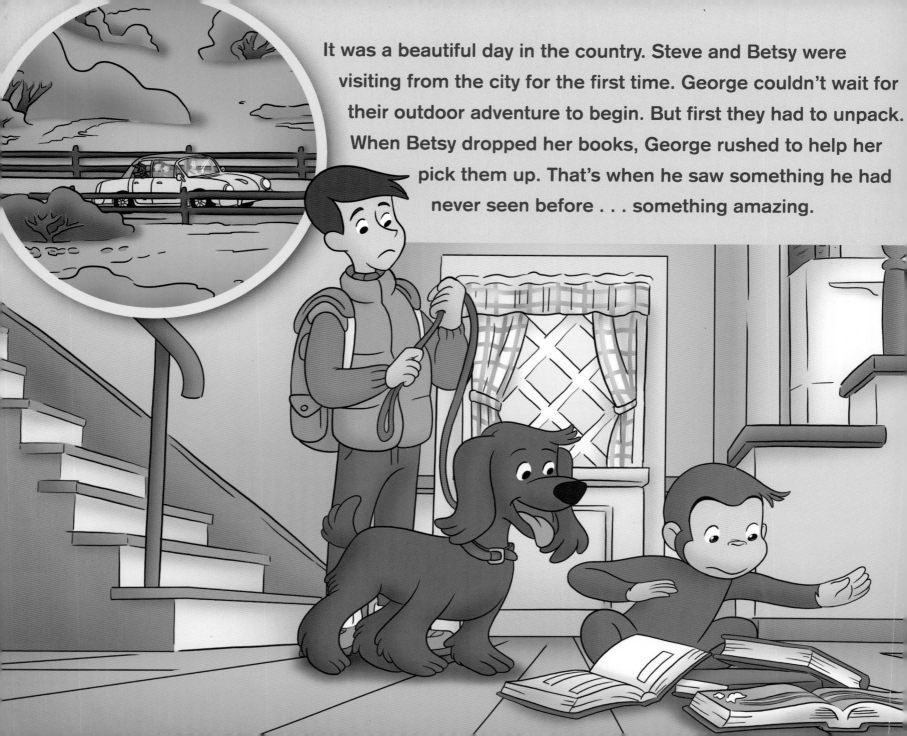

"That's a rainbow, George!" said Betsy. "See the pot of gold at the end? And the leprechaun? Rainbows are always the same seven colors: red, orange, yellow, green, blue, indigo, and violet."

"Rainbows are created by the sun and the rain," Betsy explained, "but I can make a rainbow without either. Wanna see?" A rainbow inside? George could hardly wait! Betsy used scissors to cut a slit in the center of a sheet of paper. Then she taped the paper over a flashlight and shined the light through a fishbowl full of water.

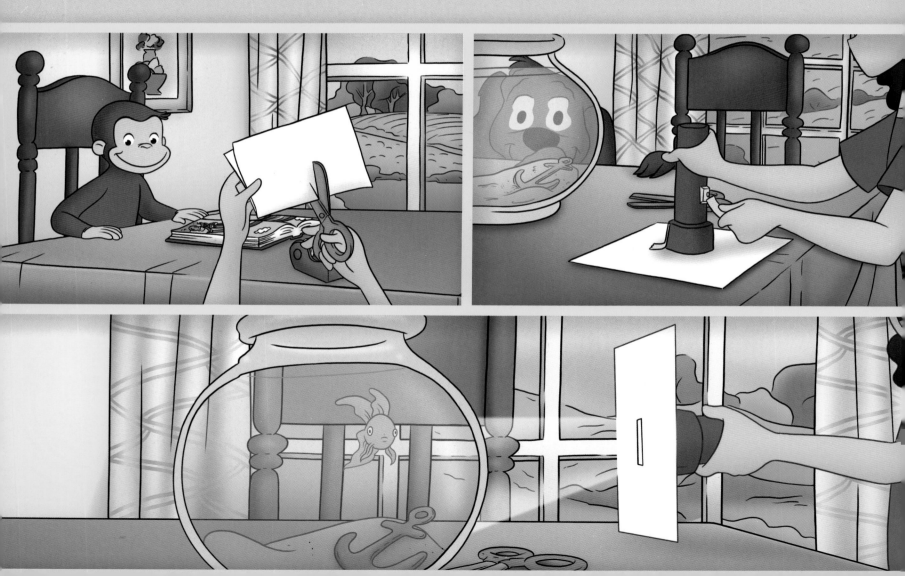

"The flashlight is like a sunbeam and the water is like a giant raindrop. The light shines through the water, and behold!" Betsy said proudly. "A rainbow!"

George thought Betsy's rainbow was nice, but there was no leprechaun or pot of gold. George wondered if he would ever see a real rainbow that spanned the whole sky. Have you?

He looked out the window. White, fluffy clouds floated by. "Looks like a nice day." said the man with the yellow hat.

Meanwhile the man helped Steve prepare for a hike.

"Have you ever seen any wild animals?" Steve asked.

"We've got skunks and deer. I've even seen a moose or two," the man replied.

"A moose!" Steve said. "Now, there's something you don't see in the city."

Did you know . . .

plants and animals rely on the weather? The right balance of temperature, rain, and sunshine makes plants grow so people and animals will have food to eat. Too much water destroys a plant's roots. Without enough water, they dry out. All of these things—land, weather, living things—make up an environment. Not every environment is right for every animal. Moose prefer quiet mountain environments. That's why you won't find them in the city. What other animals might you find outside the city?

Did you know . . .

that thunder and lightning are partners? When there is thunder, there is always lightning, even if we can't see it. When a bolt of lightning shoots through a cloud toward the ground, it creates an open space in the air. When the light vanishes, the opening is closed. This creates a loud BOOM sound. That's thunder! We may not *see* lightning if a storm is too far away. But when a storm is close, we always see lightning before we hear thunder. Can you guess why? Because light travels faster than sound.

At last it was time for their hike. Outside the sun was shining, but the temperature was cooler, and more clouds were rolling in.

"I'm driving into town to get food for dinner," said the man. Just then, thunder grumbled low in the distance. "If it rains, head home," he added. "George knows the way."

George led them into the forest.

"I'm not leaving without a picture of a moose," Steve said. Just then, he felt a raindrop. "Oh no. Not rain! Do we have to go back already?"

"I don't think so," Betsy said. "It's probably going to stop soon. Look! The sun is already peeking through the clouds."

Sunlight *and* rain at the same time? Could this be George's lucky day? Sure enough, when he turned around there was a huge, colorful rainbow arcing across the sky. His wish had come true!

"That's the biggest rainbow I've ever seen," said Betsy.

George was excited to have found a rainbow. But he couldn't see the pot of gold from here.

Steve was excited, too. "I'm climbing this tree to take a picture of the rainbow," he said, scampering high into its branches.

George needed a better view too. He knew if he was going to find the pot of gold or see a leprechaun, he needed to get closer. So what do you think he did? George ran off in search of the rainbow's end with Charkie close behind. "Charkie! George! Wait!" Betsy yelled, chasing them through the rain.

When Betsy finally caught up with them, George tried to explain that he had wanted to reach the pot of gold. But no matter how far or fast he and Charkie ran, the rainbow only got farther away.

Did you know . . .

a rainbow is an "optical illusion"? That's a trick of the eye that makes us see something that isn't really there. We can see a rainbow, but we can never touch one, because it is made only of light.

Test it out!

You'll need . . .

- a pencil
- your hand
- an audience

Hold the pencil lightly between your thumb and index finger. Gently move your arm up and down. Notice how the pencil appears to bend like rubber? That's an optical illusion! The pencil does not bend like rubber—it only looks like it does.

"The leprechaun with a pot of gold is just a fairy tale," said Betsy. "But I guess it couldn't hurt to look just in case, could it, Steve?" But Steve was nowhere in sight. "He'll catch up with us," said Betsy. "Let's keep going."

They hadn't gone far when something small and green hopped through the bushes. Could it be the leprechaun? George thought he must be getting close to the pot of gold now!

But it was only a green frog. Usually George would be happy to meet a frog, but it was no leprechaun.

George wasn't disappointed for long, though, because the frog had led him to a second rainbow!

"Sorry, George," Betsy said. "That's not another rainbow—it's only the reflection of the rainbow on the water. How will we keep chasing the rainbow now? We need to cross the river."

Did you know . . .

there is such a thing as a secondary rainbow? When light does not escape the raindrop after being reflected the first time, it reflects off the raindrop's surface a second time, creating what looks like a double rainbow. But most of the light is already used up, so the second rainbow will be harder to see.

If you're near a body of water when there's a rainbow in the sky, you might also see a "reflected rainbow" like George did. Just as a raindrop reflects light, a lake, pond, or even a puddle can reflect light too!

Just then, Charkie darted through the bushes after the frog and found what they needed most. A boat!

"Uh-oh," Betsy said as they floated away. "How will Steve ever catch up with us now?"

Meanwhile, Steve realized he was all alone.

"Charkie! Betsy! George? Where are you?" he called.

Suddenly something moved in the bushes. What do you think it was?

"A moose!" Steve shouted, snapping a picture. But the moose didn't like Steve's loud voice, or his camera. Steve was scared. He was about to call for help when he heard a voice.

"Back away from the moose slowly," the boy said. It was George's friend Bill. He knew a lot about the wilderness. "And whatever you do, don't frighten it," Bill added. The moose walked off into the forest.

Did you know . . .

that moose are good swimmers? When temperatures rise, they keep cool in mountain lakes and streams. Moose are also heavy and fast. They weigh up to 1,500 pounds (680 kg) and can run thirty-five miles (56 km) per hour. If they feel threatened, they are considered more dangerous than grizzly bears!

When the coast was clear, Bill introduced himself. "I'm Bill. And you're lucky I found you. Moose can be dangerous!"

"Hey, I'm Steve," he said to Bill. "Since you're so good at finding things, maybe you can help me find my sister and our friend George?"

"I know George," Bill said. "Follow me. I saw his friend in town. He'll help us."

"Steve!" said the man. "Where are Betsy, Charkie, and George?"

"We got separated in the woods," Steve said. "I don't know where they went."

Just then something sparkly caught his eye. More rainbows!

"Oh yeah!" Steve remembered. "George saw a rainbow right before they ran off."

"If I know George, I bet he went to find the gold at the end of the rainbow. I have an idea to help him get home," the man said.

When George, Betsy, and Charkie reached the shore, daylight was fading and so was the rainbow.

George knew they needed to get home before dark. There was only one problem: he didn't know where they were anymore.

Suddenly, Charkie began to bark. Something was glowing from the end of the rainbow! It must be their pot of gold! George, Betsy, and Charkie raced toward the light.

"George! Over here," called the man with the yellow . . . balloon!
He was standing on the roof of their house holding a bright,
shiny balloon that was wearing a very familiar yellow hat.

George was happy to be home with his friends. There was no pot of gold, but he knew he had found the *real* treasure at the end of the rainbow.

Measuring Rainfall

How much water falls during a rain shower?
You can measure it by making a rain gauge.

You will need . . .
- a clear jar
- a ruler

Directions:

Place your jar outside, where it can collect water when it starts to rain. Once the shower is over, use the ruler to measure how much water you collected.

Explore further:

Rain is caused by the earth's water cycle. There are three parts:

- **Evaporation:** Heat from the sun causes water in lakes, streams, and oceans to turn from a liquid to a gas. This gas, also called water vapor, rises into the sky, forming clouds.

- **Condensation:** Water vapor begins to cool and becomes liquid again.

- **Precipitation:** Liquid falls from the sky as rain, snow, sleet, or even hail. The sun evaporates the precipitation and the cycle begins again.

How Close Is a Thunderstorm?

Did you know you could use time to figure out if a thunderstorm is getting closer or farther from where you are?

You will need . . .

- **your eyes**
- **your ears**
- **a thunderstorm**

Directions:

From a safe place indoors, watch the sky for a flash of lightning. Count the number of seconds that pass until you hear a clap of thunder. Remember that number. (Hint: You can use a watch, or count one-Missisippi, two-Missisippi, and so on.) At the next flash of lightning, count the seconds until you hear thunder again. Repeat this process several times. If the amount of time between lightning flashes and thunderclaps gets longer, the storm is moving away from you. If the amount of time between lightning and thunder gets shorter, the storm is getting closer.

aking Rainbows

Did you know that there are two types of colors?

Primary colors are red, blue, and yellow.

Secondary colors are orange, purple, and green.
Secondary colors are created when primary colors
are mixed together, like this:

These combinations create the colors of the rainbow!

Test It Out!

You will need . . .

- a shallow bowl or pie plate
- whole milk or half-and-half (room temperature works best)
- red, yellow, and blue food coloring
- liquid dish soap
- a cotton swab

1. Pour enough milk to cover the bottom of the bowl.

2. Near the center of the bowl, add three drops of red food coloring to the milk, keeping the drops in one spot. Repeat this step with the yellow and blue food coloring to create a triangle.

3. Squeeze a drop of dish soap onto one end of your cotton swab, and carefully place the soapy end directly into the milk in the center your triangle. Hold it there for ten seconds. What happens? Add another drop of soap to your cotton swab and try dipping it into different spots. How many colors do you see?